COMMON CO[RE]
MIDDLE SCHOOL WORKBOOK
GRADE 8

Common Core Middle School Workbook Grade 8

First Edition - 04/02/15

Andrew Frinkle © Copyright 2015

TABLE OF CONTENTS:

READING: LITERATURE

READING: LITERATURE

Key Ideas and Details:

CCSS.ELA-LITERACY.RL.8.1

Cite the textual evidence that most strongly supports an analysis of what the text says explicitly as well as inferences drawn from the text.

CCSS.ELA-LITERACY.RL.8.2

Determine a theme or central idea of a text and analyze its development over the course of the text, including its relationship to the characters, setting, and plot; provide an objective summary of the text.

CCSS.ELA-LITERACY.RL.8.3

Analyze how particular lines of dialogue or incidents in a story or drama propel the action, reveal aspects of a character, or provoke a decision.

Craft and Structure:

CCSS.ELA-LITERACY.RL.8.4

Determine the meaning of words and phrases as they are used in a text, including figurative and connotative meanings; analyze the impact of specific word choices on meaning and tone, including analogies or allusions to other texts.

CCSS.ELA-LITERACY.RL.8.5

Compare and contrast the structure of two or more texts and analyze how the differing structure of each text contributes to its meaning and style.

CCSS.ELA-LITERACY.RL.8.6

Analyze how differences in the points of view of the characters and the audience or reader (e.g., created through the use of dramatic irony) create such effects as suspense or humor.

GRADE 8 STANDARDS

READING: LITERATURE

Integration of Knowledge and Ideas:

CCSS.ELA-LITERACY.RL.7.7

Compare and contrast a written story, drama, or poem to its audio, filmed, staged, or multimedia version, analyzing the effects of techniques unique to each medium (e.g., lighting, sound, color, or camera focus and angles in a film).

CCSS.ELA-LITERACY.RL.7.8

(RL.7.8 not applicable to literature)

CCSS.ELA-LITERACY.RL.7.9

Compare and contrast a fictional portrayal of a time, place, or character and a historical account of the same period as a means of understanding how authors of fiction use or alter history.

Range of Reading and Level of Text Complexity:

CCSS.ELA-LITERACY.RL.8.10

By the end of the year, read and comprehend literature, including stories, dramas, and poems, at the high end of grades 6-8 text complexity band independently and proficiently.

GRADE 8 WORKSHEETS: RL.8.1

NAME:

SCORE:

SOURCE:

INFERENCE/ANALYSIS: _____

_____

TEXT EVIDENCE: _____

_____

TEXT EVIDENCE: _____

_____

INFERENCE/ANALYSIS: _____

_____

TEXT EVIDENCE: _____

_____

TEXT EVIDENCE: _____

_____

RL.8.1: *Cite the textual evidence that most strongly supports an analysis of what the text says explicitly as well as inferences drawn from the text.*

MIDDLE SCHOOL COMMON CORE ASSESSMENTS (C) 2015 Andrew Frinkle

GRADE 8 WORKSHEETS: RL.8.2

NAME:

SCORE:

SOURCE:

THEME: _____

HOW DOES THE THEME DEVELOP THROUGH THE TEXT? _____

HOW IS THE THEME RELATED TO THE CHARACTER, SETTING, AND PLOT?

SUMMARY: _____

RL.8.2: *Determine a theme or central idea of a text and analyze its development over the course of the text, including its relationship to the characters, setting, and plot; provide an objective summary of the text.*

NAME:

SCORE:

SOURCE:

DIALOGUE/EVENT(S):

_____

_____

_____

_____

_____

HOW DO THE DIALOGUE OR THE EVENT(S) ABOVE AFFECT THE STORY?

_____

_____

_____

_____

_____

_____

RL.8.3: _Analyze how particular lines of dialogue or incidents in a story or drama propel the action, reveal aspects of a character, or provoke a decision._

NAME:

SCORE:

SOURCE:

WORD: **MEANING:**

#1 _____ = _____

#2 _____ = _____

#3 _____ = _____

#4 _____ = _____

#5 _____ = _____

WHAT IMPACT DO THESE WORDS/PHRASES HAVE ON THE TEXT?

_____

_____

WHAT OTHER STORIES HAVE SIMILAR THEMES AND VOCABULARY?

_____

RL.8.4: *Determine the meaning of words and phrases as they are used in a text, including figurative and connotative meanings; analyze the impact of specific word choices on meaning and tone, including analogies or allusions to other texts.*

GRADE 8 WORKSHEETS: RL.8.5

NAME:

SCORE:

SOURCE 1:

STYLE:

SOURCE 2:

STYLE:

HOW ARE THE STRUCTURES SIMILAR?

_____

_____

_____

_____

_____

HOW ARE THE STRUCTURES DIFFERENT?

_____

_____

_____

_____

_____

HOW DOES THE STRUCTURE OF EACH ADD TO THE MEANING/STYLE OF THE PIECE?

_____

_____

RL.8.5: _Compare and contrast the structure of two or more texts and analyze how the differing structure of each text contributes to its meaning and style._

GRADE 8 WORKSHEETS: RL.8.6

NAME:

SCORE:

SOURCE:

NARRATOR/SPEAKER OF TEXT:

POINT OF VIEW EXAMPLES:

_____

_____

_____

HOW IS THE NARRATOR/SPEAKER'S POINT OF VIEW DIFFERENT FROM YOURS?

_____

_____

WHAT EFFECTS DOES THE DIFFERENCE OF POINTS OF VIEW CREATE?

_____

_____

_____

RL.8.6: Analyze how differences in the points of view of the characters and the audience or reader (e.g., created through the use of dramatic irony) create such effects as suspense or humor.

GRADE 8 WORKSHEETS: RL.8.7

NAME:

SCORE:

SOURCE 1:

SOURCE 2:

HOW ARE THE VERSIONS THE SAME?

_____

_____

_____

_____

_____

HOW ARE THE VERSIONS DIFFERENT?

_____

_____

_____

_____

_____

PROVIDE A CRITIQUE OF THE LIVE/FILMED VERSION VS. THE TEXT VERSION:

_____

_____

_____

RL.8.7: Analyze the extent to which a filmed or live production of a story or drama stays faithful to or departs from the text or script, evaluating the choices made by the director or actors.

GRADE 8 WORKSHEETS: RL.8.9

NAME:

SCORE:

SOURCE:

RELATED/SIMILAR WORKS: **WHAT IS SIMILAR ABOUT THEM?**

_____   _____

_____   _____

_____   _____

_____   _____

HOW DID THE AUTHOR CHANGE OR ADAPT THE SIMILAR WORKS?

_____

_____

HOW SUCCESSFUL WAS THE AUTHOR IN MIXING THE OLD AND NEW?

_____

_____

RL.8.9: Analyze how a modern work of fiction draws on themes, patterns of events, or character types from myths, traditional stories, or religious works such as the Bible, including describing how the material is rendered new.

NAME: **SCORE:**

STORY: **GENRE:**

#1 _____   _____

STORY: **GENRE:**

#2 _____   _____

STORY: **GENRE:**

#3 _____   _____

STORY: **GENRE:**

#4 _____   _____

STORY: **GENRE:**

#5 _____   _____

STORY: **GENRE:**

#6 _____   _____

STORY: **GENRE:**

#7 _____   _____

RL.8.10: *By the end of the year, read and comprehend literature, including stories, dramas, and poems, at the high end of grades 6-8 text complexity band independently and proficiently.*

READING: INFORMATIONAL TEXT

READING: INFORMATIONAL TEXT

Key Ideas and Details:

CCSS.ELA-LITERACY.RI.8.1

Cite the textual evidence that most strongly supports an analysis of what the text says explicitly as well as inferences drawn from the text.

CCSS.ELA-LITERACY.RI.8.2

Determine a central idea of a text and analyze its development over the course of the text, including its relationship to supporting ideas; provide an objective summary of the text.

CCSS.ELA-LITERACY.RI.8.3

Analyze how a text makes connections among and distinctions between individuals, ideas, or events (e.g., through comparisons, analogies, or categories).

Craft and Structure:

CCSS.ELA-LITERACY.RI.8.4

Determine the meaning of words and phrases as they are used in a text, including figurative, connotative, and technical meanings; analyze the impact of specific word choices on meaning and tone, including analogies or allusions to other texts.

CCSS.ELA-LITERACY.RI.8.5

Analyze in detail the structure of a specific paragraph in a text, including the role of particular sentences in developing and refining a key concept.

CCSS.ELA-LITERACY.RI.8.6

Determine an author's point of view or purpose in a text and analyze how the author acknowledges and responds to conflicting evidence or viewpoints.

READING: INFORMATIONAL TEXT

Integration of Knowledge and Ideas:

CCSS.ELA-LITERACY.RI.8.7

Evaluate the advantages and disadvantages of using different mediums (e.g., print or digital text, video, multimedia) to present a particular topic or idea.

CCSS.ELA-LITERACY.RI.8.8

Delineate and evaluate the argument and specific claims in a text, assessing whether the reasoning is sound and the evidence is relevant and sufficient; recognize when irrelevant evidence is introduced.

CCSS.ELA-LITERACY.RI.8.9

Analyze a case in which two or more texts provide conflicting information on the same topic and identify where the texts disagree on matters of fact or interpretation.

Range of Reading and Level of Text Complexity:

CCSS.ELA-LITERACY.RI.7.10

By the end of the year, read and comprehend literary nonfiction at the high end of the grades 6-8 text complexity band independently and proficiently.

GRADE 8 WORKSHEETS: RI.8.1

NAME:

SCORE:

SOURCE:

INFERENCE/ANALYSIS: _____

_____

TEXT EVIDENCE: _____

_____

TEXT EVIDENCE: _____

_____

INFERENCE/ANALYSIS: _____

_____

TEXT EVIDENCE: _____

_____

TEXT EVIDENCE: _____

_____

RI.8.1: Cite the textual evidence that most strongly supports an analysis of what the text says explicitly as well as inferences drawn from the text.

GRADE 8 WORKSHEETS: RI.8.2

NAME:

SCORE:

SOURCE:

CENTRAL IDEA: _____

_____

_____

HOW DOES THIS IDEA DEVELOP? _____

_____

CENTRAL IDEA: _____

_____

_____

HOW DOES THIS IDEA DEVELOP? _____

_____

SUMMARY: _____

_____

_____

_____

RI.8.2: *Determine a central idea of a text and analyze its development over the course of the text, including its relationship to supporting ideas; provide an objective summary of the text.*

GRADE 8 WORKSHEETS: RI.8.3

NAME:

SCORE:

SOURCE:

EVENTS: _____

_____

CHARACTERS: _____

_____

IDEAS: _____

_____

HOW ARE ELEMENTS CONNECTED TO OR DISTINGUISHED FROM EACH OTHER?

_____

_____

_____

_____

_____

RI.8.3: _Analyze how a text makes connections among and distinctions between individuals, ideas, or events (e.g., through comparisons, analogies, or categories)._

GRADE 8 WORKSHEETS: RI.8.4

NAME:

SCORE:

SOURCE:

WORD: **MEANING:**

#1 _____ = _____

#2 _____ = _____

#3 _____ = _____

#4 _____ = _____

#5 _____ = _____

WHAT IMPACT DO THESE WORDS/PHRASES HAVE ON THE TEXT?

_____

_____

WHAT OTHER TEXTS HAVE SIMILAR THEMES AND VOCABULARY?

_____

RI.8.4: *Determine the meaning of words and phrases as they are used in a text, including figurative, connotative, and technical meanings; analyze the impact of specific word choices on meaning and tone, including analogies or allusions to other texts.*

GRADE 8 WORKSHEETS: RI.8.5

NAME:

SCORE:

SOURCE:

HOW IS THE PARAGRAPH STRUCTURED?

_____

_____

_____

_____

_____

CHOOSE A SENTENCE & EXPLAIN HOW THE SENTENCE HELPS DEVELOP THE CONCEPT:

_____

_____

_____

CHOOSE A SENTENCE & EXPLAIN HOW THE SENTENCE HELPS DEVELOP THE CONCEPT:

_____

_____

_____

RI.8.5: _Analyze in detail the structure of a specific paragraph in a text, including the role of particular sentences in developing and refining a key concept._

NAME:

SCORE:

SOURCE:

POINT OF VIEW OR PURPOSE:

EXAMPLES:

#1 _____

#2 _____

#3 _____

#4 _____

#5 _____

HOW DOES THE AUTHOR RESPOND TO OTHER VIEWPOINTS? _____

_____

_____

RI.8.6: Determine an author's point of view or purpose in a text and analyze how the author acknowledges and responds to conflicting evidence or viewpoints.

GRADE 8 WORKSHEETS: RI.8.7

NAME:

SCORE:

TOPIC:

SOURCE 1:

SOURCE 2:

MEDIUM:

MEDIUM:

PROS/CONS:

_____

_____

_____

_____

_____

_____

PROS/CONS:

_____

_____

_____

_____

_____

_____

RI.8.7: _Evaluate the advantages and disadvantages of using different mediums (e.g., print or digital text, video, multimedia) to present a particular topic or idea._

GRADE 8 WORKSHEETS: RI.8.8

NAME:

SCORE:

SOURCE:

ARGUMENT:

SUPPORTED CLAIMS:

_____

_____

_____

_____

_____

UNSUPPORTED CLAIMS:

_____

_____

_____

_____

_____

IS THE ARGUMENT MOSTLY SUPPORTED OR UNSUPPORTED BY FACTS?

_____

_____

RI.8.8: *Delineate and evaluate the argument and specific claims in a text, assessing whether the reasoning is sound and the evidence is relevant and sufficient; recognize when irrelevant evidence is introduced.*

NAME:

SCORE:

SOURCE 1:

SOURCE 2:

AGREED UPON INFORMATION:

_____

_____

_____

_____

_____

CONFLICTING INFORMATION:

_____

_____

_____

_____

_____

WHERE WAS THE INFORMATION DISAGREED UPON BECAUSE OF INTERPRETATION?

_____

_____

_____

RI.8.9: Analyze a case in which two or more texts provide conflicting information on the same topic and identify where the texts disagree on matters of fact or interpretation.

NAME:

SCORE:

TEXT:

GENRE:

#1 _____ _____

TEXT:

GENRE:

#2 _____ _____

TEXT:

GENRE:

#3 _____ _____

TEXT:

GENRE:

#4 _____ _____

TEXT:

GENRE:

#5 _____ _____

TEXT:

GENRE:

#6 _____ _____

TEXT:

GENRE:

#7 _____ _____

RI.8.10: By the end of the year, read and comprehend literary nonfiction at the high end of the grades 6-8 text complexity band independently and proficiently.

WRITING

WRITING

Text Types and Purposes:

CCSS.ELA-LITERACY.W.8.1

Write arguments to support claims with clear reasons and relevant evidence

- CCSS.ELA-LITERACY.W.8.1.A

Introduce claim(s), acknowledge and distinguish the claim(s) from alternate or opposing claims, and organize the reasons and evidence logically.

- CCSS.ELA-LITERACY.W.8.1.B

Support claim(s) with logical reasoning and relevant evidence, using accurate, credible sources and demonstrating an understanding of the topic or text.

- CCSS.ELA-LITERACY.W.8.1.C

Use words, phrases, and clauses to create cohesion and clarify the relationships among claim(s), counterclaims, reasons, and evidence.

- CCSS.ELA-LITERACY.W.8.1.D

Establish and maintain a formal style.

- CCSS.ELA-LITERACY.W.8.1.E

Provide a concluding statement or section that follows from and supports the argument presented.

WRITING

Text Types and Purposes (continued):

CCSS.ELA-LITERACY.W.8.2

Write informative/explanatory texts to examine a topic and convey ideas, concepts, and information through the selection, organization, and analysis of relevant content.

- CCSS.ELA-LITERACY.W.8.2.A

Introduce a topic clearly, previewing what is to follow; organize ideas, concepts, and information into broader categories; include formatting (e.g., headings), graphics (e.g., charts, tables), and multimedia when useful to aiding comprehension.

- CCSS.ELA-LITERACY.W.8.2.B

Develop the topic with relevant, well-chosen facts, definitions, concrete details, quotations, or other information and examples.

- CCSS.ELA-LITERACY.W.8.2.C

Use appropriate and varied transitions to create cohesion and clarify the relationships among ideas and concepts.

- CCSS.ELA-LITERACY.W.8.2.D

Use precise language and domain-specific vocabulary to inform about or explain the topic.

- CCSS.ELA-LITERACY.W.8.2.E

Establish and maintain a formal style.

- CCSS.ELA-LITERACY.W.8.2.F

Provide a concluding statement or section that follows from and supports the information or explanation presented.

WRITING

Text Types and Purposes (continued):

CCSS.ELA-LITERACY.W.8.3

Write narratives to develop real or imagined experiences or events using effective technique, relevant descriptive details, and well-structured event sequences.

- CCSS.ELA-LITERACY.W.8.3.A

Engage and orient the reader by establishing a context and point of view and introducing a narrator and/or characters; organize an event sequence that unfolds naturally and logically.

- CCSS.ELA-LITERACY.W.8.3.B

Use narrative techniques, such as dialogue, pacing, description, and reflection, to develop experiences, events, and/or characters.

- CCSS.ELA-LITERACY.W.8.3.C

Use a variety of transition words, phrases, and clauses to convey sequence, signal shifts from one time frame or setting to another, and show the relationships among experiences and events.

- CCSS.ELA-LITERACY.W.8.3.D

Use precise words and phrases, relevant descriptive details, and sensory language to capture the action and convey experiences and events.

- CCSS.ELA-LITERACY.W.8.3.E

Provide a conclusion that follows from and reflects on the narrated experiences or events.

WRITING

Production and Distribution of Writing:

CCSS.ELA-LITERACY.W.8.4

Produce clear and coherent writing in which the development, organization, and style are appropriate to task, purpose, and audience. (Grade-specific expectations for writing types are defined in standards 1-3 above.)

CCSS.ELA-LITERACY.W.8.5

With some guidance and support from peers and adults, develop and strengthen writing as needed by planning, revising, editing, rewriting, or trying a new approach, focusing on how well purpose and audience have been addressed. (Editing for conventions should demonstrate command of Language standards 1-3 up to and including grade 8 here.)

CCSS.ELA-LITERACY.W.8.6

Use technology, including the Internet, to produce and publish writing and present the relationships between information and ideas efficiently as well as to interact and collaborate with others.

WRITING

Research to Build and Present Knowledge:

CCSS.ELA-LITERACY.W.8.7

Conduct short research projects to answer a question (including a self-generated question), drawing on several sources and generating additional related, focused questions that allow for multiple avenues of exploration.

CCSS.ELA-LITERACY.W.8.8

Gather relevant information from multiple print and digital sources, using search terms effectively; assess the credibility and accuracy of each source; and quote or paraphrase the data and conclusions of others while avoiding plagiarism and following a standard format for citation.

CCSS.ELA-LITERACY.W.8.9

Draw evidence from literary or informational texts to support analysis, reflection, and research.

- CCSS.ELA-LITERACY.W.8.9.A

Apply *grade 8 Reading standards* to literature (e.g., "Analyze how a modern work of fiction draws on themes, patterns of events, or character types from myths, traditional stories, or religious works such as the Bible, including describing how the material is rendered new").

- CCSS.ELA-LITERACY.W.8.9.B

Apply *grade 8 Reading standards* to literary nonfiction (e.g., "Delineate and evaluate the argument and specific claims in a text, assessing whether the reasoning is sound and the evidence is relevant and sufficient; recognize when irrelevant evidence is introduced").

WRITING

Range of Writing:

CCSS.ELA-LITERACY.W.8.10

Write routinely over extended time frames (time for research, reflection, and revision) and shorter time frames (a single sitting or a day or two) for a range of discipline-specific tasks, purposes, and audiences.

GRADE 8 WORKSHEETS: W.8.1.A-E (page 1)

NAME:

SCORE:

ARGUMENT FOR:

_____

_____

_____

SUPPORT:

_____

_____

_____

ARGUMENT AGAINST:

_____

_____

SUPPORT:

_____

_____

_____

CONCLUSION:

_____

_____

_____

W.8.1.A-E: _Write arguments to support claims with clear reasons and relevant evidence. Introduce claim(s), acknowledge and distinguish the claim(s) from alternate or opposing claims, and organize the reasons and evidence logically. Support claim(s) with logical reasoning and relevant evidence, using accurate, credible sources and demonstrating an understanding of the topic or text. Use words, phrases, and clauses to create cohesion and clarify the relationships among claim(s), counterclaims, reasons, and evidence. Establish and maintain a formal style. Provide a concluding statement or section that follows from and supports the argument presented._

NAME:

SCORE:

TITLE:

_____

_____

_____

_____

_____

_____

_____

_____

_____

_____

_____

_____

GRADE 8 WORKSHEETS: W.8.2.A-F (page 1)

NAME:

SCORE:

TITLE:

TOPIC/MAIN IDEA: _____

_____

SOURCES: _____

_____

SUPPORTING MEDIA: _____

_____

NOTES: _____

_____

_____

_____

_____

W.8.2.A-F: *Write informative/explanatory texts to examine a topic and convey ideas, concepts, and information through the selection, organization, and analysis of relevant content. Introduce a topic clearly, previewing what is to follow; organize ideas, concepts, and information into broader categories; include formatting (e.g., headings), graphics (e.g., charts, tables), and multimedia when useful to aiding comprehension. Develop the topic with relevant, well-chosen facts, definitions, concrete details, quotations, or other information and examples. Use appropriate and varied transitions to create cohesion and clarify the relationships among ideas and concepts. Use precise language and domain-specific vocabulary to inform about or explain the topic. Establish and maintain a formal style. Provide a concluding statement or section that follows from and supports the information or explanation presented.*

NAME:

SCORE:

TITLE:

_____

_____

_____

_____

_____

_____

_____

_____

_____

_____

_____

*ADD GRAPHICS AND SUPPORTING MULTIMEDIA IF POSSIBLE

W.8.2.A-F: *SEE PAGE 1 FOR STANDARDS AND EXPECTATIONS*

NAME:

SCORE:

TITLE:

STORY TOPIC: _____

_____

CHARACTERS:

EVENT: _____

_____

EVENT: _____

_____

EVENT: _____

_____

CONCLUSION: _____

_____

W.8.3.A-E: Write narratives to develop real or imagined experiences or events using effective technique, relevant descriptive details, and well-structured event sequences. Engage and orient the reader by establishing a context and point of view and introducing a narrator and/or characters; organize an event sequence that unfolds naturally and logically. Use narrative techniques, such as dialogue, pacing, description, and reflection, to develop experiences, events, and/or characters. Use a variety of transition words, phrases, and clauses to convey sequence, signal shifts from one time frame or setting to another, and show the relationships among experiences and events. Use precise words and phrases, relevant descriptive details, and sensory language to capture the action and convey experiences and events. Provide a conclusion that follows from and reflects on the narrated experiences or events.

NAME:

SCORE:

TITLE:

_____

_____

_____

_____

_____

_____

_____

_____

_____

_____

_____

_____

_____

W.8.3.A-E: SEE PAGE 1 FOR STANDARDS AND EXPECTATIONS

NAME:

SCORE:

TITLE:

_____

_____

_____

_____

_____

_____

_____

_____

_____

_____

_____

W.8.3.A-E: SEE PAGE 1 FOR STANDARDS AND EXPECTATIONS

NAME:

SCORE:

TITLE:

PURPOSE:

AUDIENCE:

_____

_____

_____

_____

_____

_____

_____

_____

_____

W.8.4: _Produce clear and coherent writing in which the development, organization, and style are appropriate to task, purpose, and audience._

GRADE 8 WORKSHEETS: W.8.5 (page 1)

NAME:

SCORE:

TITLE:

ROUGH DRAFT: _____

_____

_____

_____

_____

_____

_____

_____

_____

_____

_____

_____

EDITED BY:

W.8.5: With some guidance and support from peers and adults, develop and strengthen writing as needed by planning, revising, editing, rewriting, or trying a new approach, focusing on how well purpose and audience have been addressed. (Editing for conventions should demonstrate command of Language standards 1-3 up to and including grade 8.)

TITLE:

FINAL DRAFT:

_____

_____

_____

_____

_____

_____

_____

_____

_____

_____

_____

_____

_____

NAME:

SCORE:

TOPIC:

SOURCE 1:

NOTES FROM SOURCE 1:

_____

_____

_____

SOURCE 2:

NOTES FROM SOURCE 2:

_____

_____

_____

HOW DID YOU USE TECHNOLOGY AND/OR THE INTERNET FOR WRITING?

_____

_____

W.8.6: Use technology, including the Internet, to produce and publish writing and present the relationships between information and ideas efficiently as well as to interact and collaborate with others.

NAME:

SCORE:

TITLE:

ROUGH DRAFT: _____

_____

_____

_____

_____

_____

_____

_____

_____

_____

_____

_____

*USE YOUR NOTES AND ROUGH DRAFT TO TYPE A PAPER

W.8.6: SEE PAGE 1 FOR STANDARDS AND EXPECTATIONS

NAME:

SCORE:

WORKS CITED/BIBLIOGRAPHY

SOURCE:

SOURCE:

SOURCE:

SOURCE:

NAME:

SCORE:

RESEARCH QUESTION:

SOURCE 1:

NOTES FROM SOURCE 1: _____

_____

SOURCE 2:

NOTES FROM SOURCE 2: _____

_____

SOURCE 3:

NOTES FROM SOURCE 3: _____

_____

W.8.7: Conduct short research projects to answer a question (including a self-generated question), drawing on several sources and generating additional related, focused questions that allow for multiple avenues of exploration.

GRADE 8 WORKSHEETS: W.8.7 (page 2)

NAME:

SCORE:

TITLE:

RESEARCH: _____

_____

_____

_____

_____

_____

_____

_____

_____

_____

_____

FOLLOW-UP RESEARCH QUESTIONS:

_____

_____

W.8.7: SEE PAGE 1 FOR STANDARDS AND EXPECTATIONS

MIDDLE SCHOOL COMMON CORE ASSESSMENTS (C) 2015 Andrew Frinkle

GRADE 8 WORKSHEETS: W.8.8 (page 1)

NAME:

SCORE:

TOPIC/QUESTION:

SOURCE 1:

NOTES FROM SOURCE 1:

SOURCE 2:

NOTES FROM SOURCE 2:

WHY ARE THESE SOURCES CREDIBLE?

W.8.8: *Gather relevant information from multiple print and digital sources, using search terms effectively; assess the credibility and accuracy of each source; and quote or paraphrase the data and conclusions of others while avoiding plagiarism and following a standard format for citation.*

NAME:

SCORE:

TITLE:

USE YOUR SOURCES IN A PAPER: _____

_____

_____

_____

_____

_____

_____

_____

_____

_____

_____

_____

_____

_____

NAME:

SCORE:

WORKS CITED/BIBLIOGRAPHY

SOURCE:

SOURCE:

SOURCE:

SOURCE:

GRADE 8 WORKSHEETS: W.8.9.A

NAME:

SCORE:

SOURCE:

RELATED/SIMILAR WORKS: **WHAT IS SIMILAR ABOUT THEM?**

_____   _____

_____   _____

_____   _____

_____   _____

HOW DID THE AUTHOR CHANGE OR ADAPT THE SIMILAR WORKS?

_____

_____

_____

HOW SUCCESSFUL WAS THE AUTHOR IN MIXING THE OLD AND NEW?

_____

_____

W.8.9.A: Draw evidence from literary or informational texts to support analysis, reflection, and research. Apply grade 8 Reading standards to literature (e.g., "Analyze how a modern work of fiction draws on themes, patterns of events, or character types from myths, traditional stories, or religious works such as the Bible, including describing how the material is rendered new").

NAME:

SCORE:

SOURCE:

ARGUMENT:

SUPPORTED CLAIMS:	UNSUPPORTED CLAIMS:
_____	_____
_____	_____
_____	_____
_____	_____
_____	_____

IS THE ARGUMENT MOSTLY SUPPORTED OR UNSUPPORTED BY FACTS?

_____

_____

W.8.9.B: Draw evidence from literary or informational texts to support analysis, reflection, and research. Apply grade 8 Reading standards to literary nonfiction (e.g., "Delineate and evaluate the argument and specific claims in a text, assessing whether the reasoning is sound and the evidence is relevant and sufficient; recognize when irrelevant evidence is introduced").

NAME:

SCORE:

TITLE:	PURPOSE/GENRE:	AUDIENCE:
#1 _____	QUICK-WRITE	_____
#2 _____	QUICK-WRITE	_____
#3 _____	NARRATIVE	_____
#4 _____	INFORMATIVE	_____
#5 _____	RESEARCH	_____
#6 _____	ROUGH DRAFT	_____
#7 _____	REVISION	_____
#8 _____	_____	_____
#9 _____	_____	_____
#10 _____	_____	_____

W.8.10: *Write routinely over extended time frames (time for research, reflection, and revision) and shorter time frames (a single sitting or a day or two) for a range of discipline-specific tasks, purposes, and audiences.*

NAME:

SCORE:

GRADE 8 WORKSHEETS: BIBLIOGRAPHY

NAME:

SCORE:

WORKS CITED/BIBLIOGRAPHY

SOURCE:

SOURCE:

SOURCE:

SOURCE:

SOURCE:

GRADE 8 WORKSHEETS: WRITING LOG

NAME:

SCORE:

TITLE:	PURPOSE/GENRE:	AUDIENCE:
#1		
#2		
#3		
#4		
#5		
#6		
#7		
#8		
#9		
#10		

SPEAKING & LISTENING

SPEAKING & LISTENING

Comprehension and Collaboration:

CCSS.ELA-LITERACY.SL.8.1

Engage effectively in a range of collaborative discussions (one-on-one, in groups, and teacher-led) with diverse partners on grade 8 topics, texts, and issues, building on others' ideas and expressing their own clearly.

- CCSS.ELA-LITERACY.SL.8.1.A

Come to discussions prepared, having read or researched material under study; explicitly draw on that preparation by referring to evidence on the topic, text, or issue to probe and reflect on ideas under discussion.

- CCSS.ELA-LITERACY.SL.8.1.B

Follow rules for collegial discussions and decision-making, track progress toward specific goals and deadlines, and define individual roles as needed.

- CCSS.ELA-LITERACY.SL.8.1.C

Pose questions that connect the ideas of several speakers and respond to others' questions and comments with relevant evidence, observations, and ideas.

- CCSS.ELA-LITERACY.SL.8.1.D

Acknowledge new information expressed by others, and, when warranted, qualify or justify their own views in light of the evidence presented.

GRADE 8 STANDARDS

SPEAKING & LISTENING

Comprehension and Collaboration (continued):

CCSS.ELA-LITERACY.SL.8.2

Analyze the purpose of information presented in diverse media and formats (e.g., visually, quantitatively, orally) and evaluate the motives (e.g., social, commercial, political) behind its presentation.

CCSS.ELA-LITERACY.SL.8.3

Delineate a speaker's argument and specific claims, evaluating the soundness of the reasoning and relevance and sufficiency of the evidence and identifying when irrelevant evidence is introduced.

Presentation of Knowledge and Ideas:

CCSS.ELA-LITERACY.SL.8.4

Present claims and findings, emphasizing salient points in a focused, coherent manner with relevant evidence, sound valid reasoning, and well-chosen details; use appropriate eye contact, adequate volume, and clear pronunciation.

CCSS.ELA-LITERACY.SL.8.5

Integrate multimedia and visual displays into presentations to clarify information, strengthen claims and evidence, and add interest.

CCSS.ELA-LITERACY.SL.8.6

Adapt speech to a variety of contexts and tasks, demonstrating command of formal English when indicated or appropriate. (See grade 8 Language standards 1 and 3 here for specific expectations.)

NAME:

SCORE:

DISCUSSION TOPIC:

REFERENCES:

WHAT DID OTHERS SAY?	WHAT DID I CONTRIBUTE?
_____	_____
_____	_____
_____	_____
_____	_____
_____	_____
_____	_____

DISCUSSION SUMMARY: _____

_____

_____

SL.8.1.A-D: Engage effectively in a range of collaborative discussions (one-on-one, in groups, and teacher-led) with diverse partners on grade 8 topics, texts, and issues, building on others' ideas and expressing their own clearly. Come to discussions prepared, having read or researched material under study; explicitly draw on that preparation by referring to evidence on the topic, text, or issue to probe and reflect on ideas under discussion. Follow rules for collegial discussions and decision-making, track progress toward specific goals and deadlines, and define individual roles as needed. Pose questions that connect the ideas of several speakers and respond to others' questions and comments with relevant evidence, observations, and ideas. Acknowledge new information expressed by others, and, when warranted, qualify or justify their own views in light of the evidence presented.

NAME:

SCORE:

TOPIC:

DISCUSSION WRITE-UP: _____

_____

_____

_____

_____

_____

_____

_____

_____

_____

_____

_____

_____

_____

SL.8.1.A-D: _SEE PAGE 1 FOR STANDARDS AND EXPECTATIONS_

GRADE 8 WORKSHEETS: SL.8.2

NAME:

SCORE:

TOPIC:

SOURCE 1:

FORMAT:

MAIN IDEA(S): _____

_____

WHAT ARE THE MOTIVES BEHIND THE PRESENTATION? _____

_____

_____

_____

SOURCE 2:

FORMAT:

MAIN IDEA(S): _____

_____

WHAT ARE THE MOTIVES BEHIND THE PRESENTATION? _____

_____

_____

SL.8.2: Analyze the purpose of information presented in diverse media and formats (e.g., visually, quantitatively, orally) and evaluate the motives (e.g., social, commercial, political) behind its presentation.

GRADE 8 WORKSHEETS: SL.8.3

NAME:

SCORE:

ARGUMENT:

WHICH PARTS ARE FACT-BASED?

_____

_____

_____

_____

_____

_____

WHICH PARTS ARE OPINIONS?

_____

_____

_____

_____

_____

_____

WAS THE SUPPORT SUFFICIENT FOR THE ARGUMENT? WHY OR WHY NOT?

_____

_____

_____

_____

SL.8.3: _Delineate a speaker's argument and specific claims, evaluating the soundness of the reasoning and relevance and sufficiency of the evidence and identifying when irrelevant evidence is introduced._

NAME:

SCORE:

IDEA/ARGUMENT: _____

_____

_____

SUPPORTING DETAILS: _____

_____

SUPPORTING DETAILS: _____

_____

SUMMARY: _____

_____

_____

*PRESENT YOUR TOPIC WITH PROPER EYE CONTACT, VOLUME, & PRONUNCIATION

SL.8.4: Present claims and findings, emphasizing salient points in a focused, coherent manner with relevant evidence, sound valid reasoning, and well-chosen details; use appropriate eye contact, adequate volume, and clear pronunciation.

GRADE 8 WORKSHEETS: SL.8.5

NAME:

SCORE:

MAIN POINTS/IDEA: _____

_____

_____

_____

_____

MULTIMEDIA SOURCE:

HOW DOES THIS SOURCE SUPPORT THE TOPIC? _____

_____

MULTIMEDIA SOURCE:

HOW DOES THIS SOURCE SUPPORT THE TOPIC? _____

_____

*PRESENT YOUR TOPIC WITH MULTIMEDIA SUPPORT

SL.8.5: *Integrate multimedia and visual displays into presentations to clarify information, strengthen claims and evidence, and add interest.*

NAME:

SCORE:

SPEECH SITUATION: _____

_____

GIVE EXAMPLES OF HOW YOU ADAPTED YOUR SPEECH/LANGUAGE TO THE SITUATION:

_____

_____

_____

SPEECH SITUATION: _____

_____

GIVE EXAMPLES OF HOW YOU ADAPTED YOUR SPEECH/LANGUAGE TO THE SITUATION:

_____

_____

_____

SL.8.6: *Adapt speech to a variety of contexts and tasks, demonstrating command of formal English when indicated or appropriate. (See grade 8 Language standards 1 and 3 here for specific expectations.)*

LANGUAGE

LANGUAGE

Conventions of Standard English:

CCSS.ELA-LITERACY.L.8.1

Demonstrate command of the conventions of standard English grammar and usage when writing or speaking.

- CCSS.ELA-LITERACY.L.8.1.A

Explain the function of verbals (gerunds, participles, infinitives) in general and their function in particular sentences.

- CCSS.ELA-LITERACY.L.8.1.B

Form and use verbs in the active and passive voice.

- CCSS.ELA-LITERACY.L.8.1.C

Form and use verbs in the indicative, imperative, interrogative, conditional, and subjunctive mood.

- CCSS.ELA-LITERACY.L.8.1.D

Recognize and correct inappropriate shifts in verb voice and mood.

CCSS.ELA-LITERACY.L.8.2

Demonstrate command of the conventions of standard English capitalization, punctuation, and spelling when writing.

- CCSS.ELA-LITERACY.L.8.2.A

Use punctuation (comma, ellipsis, dash) to indicate a pause or break.

- CCSS.ELA-LITERACY.L.8.2.B

Use an ellipsis to indicate an omission.

- CCSS.ELA-LITERACY.L.8.2.C

Spell correctly.

LANGUAGE

Knowledge of Language:

CCSS.ELA-LITERACY.L.8.3

Use knowledge of language and its conventions when writing, speaking, reading, or listening.

- CCSS.ELA-LITERACY.L.8.3.A

Use verbs in the active and passive voice and in the conditional and subjunctive mood to achieve particular effects (e.g., emphasizing the actor or the action; expressing uncertainty or describing a state contrary to fact).

GRADE 8 STANDARDS

LANGUAGE

Vocabulary Acquisition and Use:

CCSS.ELA-LITERACY.L.8.4

Determine or clarify the meaning of unknown and multiple-meaning words or phrases based on *grade 8 reading and content*, choosing flexibly from a range of strategies.

- CCSS.ELA-LITERACY.L.8.4.A

Use context (e.g., the overall meaning of a sentence or paragraph; a word's position or function in a sentence) as a clue to the meaning of a word or phrase.

- CCSS.ELA-LITERACY.L.8.4.B

Use common, grade-appropriate Greek or Latin affixes and roots as clues to the meaning of a word (e.g., *precede, recede, secede*).

- CCSS.ELA-LITERACY.L.8.4.C

Consult general and specialized reference materials (e.g., dictionaries, glossaries, thesauruses), both print and digital, to find the pronunciation of a word or determine or clarify its precise meaning or its part of speech.

- CCSS.ELA-LITERACY.L.8.4.D

Verify the preliminary determination of the meaning of a word or phrase (e.g., by checking the inferred meaning in context or in a dictionary).

LANGUAGE

Vocabulary Acquisition and Use (continued):

CCSS.ELA-LITERACY.L.8.5

Demonstrate understanding of figurative language, word relationships, and nuances in word meanings.

- CCSS.ELA-LITERACY.L.8.5.A

Interpret figures of speech (e.g. verbal irony, puns) in context.

- CCSS.ELA-LITERACY.L.8.5.B

Use the relationship between particular words to better understand each of the words.

- CCSS.ELA-LITERACY.L.8.5.C

Distinguish among the connotations (associations) of words with similar denotations (definitions) (e.g., *bullheaded, willful, firm, persistent, resolute*).

CCSS.ELA-LITERACY.L.8.6

Acquire and use accurately grade-appropriate general academic and domain-specific words and phrases; gather vocabulary knowledge when considering a word or phrase important to comprehension or expression.

NAME:

SCORE:

SENTENCE:

GERUND/PARTICIPLE/INFINITIVE:

USAGE:

GERUND/PARTICIPLE/INFINITIVE:

USAGE:

GERUND/PARTICIPLE/INFINITIVE:

USAGE:

L.8.1.A-D: Demonstrate command of the conventions of standard English grammar and usage when writing or speaking. Explain the function of verbals (gerunds, participles, infinitives) in general and their function in particular sentences. Form and use verbs in the active and passive voice. Form and use verbs in the indicative, imperative, interrogative, conditional, and subjunctive mood. Recognize and correct inappropriate shifts in verb voice and mood.

NAME:

SCORE:

ORIGINAL SENTENCE(S):

SWITCH VOICES AND REWRITE THE SENTENCE(S):

ORIGINAL SENTENCE(S):

SWITCH MOODS AND REWRITE THE SENTENCE(S):

L.8.1.A-D: SEE PAGE 1 FOR STANDARDS AND EXPECTATIONS

MIDDLE SCHOOL COMMON CORE ASSESSMENTS (C) 2015 Andrew Frinkle

NAME:

SCORE:

WRITE WITH SEVERAL EXAMPLES OF CORRECT CAPITALIZATION AND SPELLING:

_____

_____

_____

_____

WRITE WITH SEVERAL EXAMPLES OF CORRECT PUNCTUATION AND SPELLING:

_____

_____

_____

_____

L.8.2.A-C: *Demonstrate command of the conventions of standard English capitalization, punctuation, and spelling when writing. Use punctuation (comma, ellipsis, dash) to indicate a pause or break. Use an ellipsis to indicate an omission. Spell correctly.*

NAME:

SCORE:

WRITE WITH CORRECT CAPITALIZATION, PUNCTUATION, AND SPELLING:

_____

_____

_____

_____

_____

_____

_____

_____

_____

_____

_____

_____

L.8.2.A-C: SEE PAGE 1 FOR STANDARDS

NAME:

SCORE:

TEXT/SPEECH SAMPLE: _____

_____

_____

REWRITE THIS TO ACCOMPLISH A DIFFERENT TASK: _____

_____

_____

WHAT EFFECT DOES THE REWRITE ACCOMPLISH?

_____

REWRITE IT AGAIN TO ACCOMPLISH ANOTHER TASK: _____

_____

_____

WHAT DIFFERENT EFFECT DOES THIS NEW REWRITE ACCOMPLISH?

_____

L.8.3: *Use knowledge of language and its conventions when writing, speaking, reading, or listening. Use verbs in the active and passive voice and in the conditional and subjunctive mood to achieve particular effects (e.g., emphasizing the actor or the action; expressing uncertainty or describing a state contrary to fact).*

NAME:

SCORE:

TEXT/SPEECH SAMPLE: _____

_____

_____

_____

_____

HOW COULD THIS SAMPLE BE CHANGED TO ACCOMPLISH SOMETHING DIFFERENT?

_____

_____

REWRITE THE SAMPLE: _____

_____

_____

_____

_____

_____

L.8.3: SEE PAGE 1 FOR STANDARDS

NAME:

SCORE:

WORD:

ROOT/AFFIXES:

GUESS:

CLUES:

ACTUAL DEFINITION:

WORD:

ROOT/AFFIXES:

GUESS:

CLUES:

ACTUAL DEFINITION:

L.8.4.A-D: Determine or clarify the meaning of unknown and multiple-meaning words or phrases based on grade 8 reading and content, choosing flexibly from a range of strategies. Use context (e.g., the overall meaning of a sentence or paragraph; a word's position or function in a sentence) as a clue to the meaning of a word or phrase. Use common, grade-appropriate Greek or Latin affixes and roots as clues to the meaning of a word (e.g., precede, recede, secede). Consult general and specialized reference materials (e.g., dictionaries, glossaries, thesauruses), both print and digital, to find the pronunciation of a word or determine or clarify its precise meaning or its part of speech. Verify the preliminary determination of the meaning of a word or phrase (e.g., by checking the inferred meaning in context or in a dictionary).

NAME:

SCORE:

WORD:

REFERENCE:

MEANING:

USE IT IN A SENTENCE:

WORD:

REFERENCE:

MEANING:

USE IT IN A SENTENCE:

WORD:

REFERENCE:

MEANING:

USE IT IN A SENTENCE:

L.8.4.A-D: *SEE PAGE 1 FOR STANDARDS AND EXPECTATIONS*

NAME:

SCORE:

WORD/PHRASE:

CLUES:

MEANING: _____

_____

WORD/PHRASE:

CLUES:

MEANING: _____

_____

WORD/PHRASE:

CLUES:

MEANING: _____

_____

L.8.5.A-C: Demonstrate understanding of figurative language, word relationships, and nuances in word meanings. Interpret figures of speech (e.g. verbal irony, puns) in context. Use the relationship between particular words to better understand each of the words. Distinguish among the connotations (associations) of words with similar denotations (definitions) (e.g., bullheaded, willful, firm, persistent, resolute).

NAME:

SCORE:

WORD/PHRASE:

MEANING:

CONNOTATION:

WORD/PHRASE:

MEANING:

CONNOTATION:

WORD/PHRASE:

MEANING:

CONNOTATION:

L.8.5.A-C: *SEE PAGE 1 FOR STANDARDS AND EXPECTATIONS*

NAME:

SCORE:

WORD/PHRASE:

USE IT CORRECTLY: _____

_____

WORD/PHRASE:

USE IT CORRECTLY: _____

_____

WORD/PHRASE:

USE IT CORRECTLY: _____

_____

WORD/PHRASE:

USE IT CORRECTLY: _____

_____

L.8.6: Acquire and use accurately grade-appropriate general academic and domain-specific words and phrases; gather vocabulary knowledge when considering a word or phrase important to comprehension or expression.

HISTORY &
SOCIAL STUDIES

GRADE 8 STANDARDS

HISTORY & SOCIAL STUDIES

Key Ideas and Details:

CCSS.ELA-LITERACY.RH.6-8.1

Cite specific textual evidence to support analysis of primary and secondary sources.

CCSS.ELA-LITERACY.RH.6-8.2

Determine the central ideas or information of a primary or secondary source; provide an accurate summary of the source distinct from prior knowledge or opinions.

CCSS.ELA-LITERACY.RH.6-8.3

Identify key steps in a text's description of a process related to history/social studies (e.g., how a bill becomes law, how interest rates are raised or lowered).

Craft and Structure:

CCSS.ELA-LITERACY.RH.6-8.4

Determine the meaning of words and phrases as they are used in a text, including vocabulary specific to domains related to history/social studies.

CCSS.ELA-LITERACY.RH.6-8.5

Describe how a text presents information (e.g., sequentially, comparatively, causally).

CCSS.ELA-LITERACY.RH.6-8.6

Identify aspects of a text that reveal an author's point of view or purpose (e.g., loaded language, inclusion or avoidance of particular facts).

GRADE 8 STANDARDS

HISTORY & SOCIAL STUDIES

Integration of Knowledge and Ideas:

CCSS.ELA-LITERACY.RH.6-8.7

Integrate visual information (e.g., in charts, graphs, photographs, videos, or maps) with other information in print and digital texts.

CCSS.ELA-LITERACY.RH.6-8.8

Distinguish among fact, opinion, and reasoned judgment in a text.

CCSS.ELA-LITERACY.RH.6-8.9

Analyze the relationship between a primary and secondary source on the same topic.

Range of Reading and Level of Text Complexity:

CCSS.ELA-LITERACY.RH.6-8.10

By the end of grade 8, read and comprehend history/social studies texts in the grades 6-8 text complexity band independently and proficiently.

NAME:

SCORE:

SOURCE 1:

IS THIS A PRIMARY OR SECONDARY SOURCE?

EVIDENCE: _____

_____

EVIDENCE: _____

_____

SOURCE 1:

IS THIS A PRIMARY OR SECONDARY SOURCE?

EVIDENCE: _____

_____

EVIDENCE: _____

_____

RH.6-8.1: *Cite specific textual evidence to support analysis of primary and secondary sources.*

GRADE 8 WORKSHEETS: RH.6-8.2

NAME:

SCORE:

SOURCE:

IS THIS A PRIMARY OR SECONDARY SOURCE?

MAIN IDEA(S): _____

_____

SUMMARY: _____

_____

_____

_____

_____

_____

_____

_____

_____

RH.6-8.2: *Determine the central ideas or information of a primary or secondary source; provide an accurate summary of the source distinct from prior knowledge or opinions.*

PROCESS:

STEPS/EVENTS:

#1 _____

#2 _____

#3 _____

#4 _____

#5 _____

#6 _____

COMMENTS: _____

_____

_____

RH.6-8.3: Identify key steps in a text's description of a process related to history/social studies (e.g., how a bill becomes law, how interest rates are raised or lowered).

GRADE 8 WORKSHEETS: RH.6-8.4

NAME: SCORE:

WORD/PHRASE:

SOURCE:

DEFINITION:

WORD/PHRASE:

SOURCE:

DEFINITION:

WORD/PHRASE:

SOURCE:

DEFINITION:

RH.6-8.4: Determine the meaning of words and phrases as they are used in a text, including vocabulary specific to domains related to history/social studies.

NAME:

SCORE:

SOURCE 1:

IN WHAT STYLE(S) IS THE MATERIAL PRESENTED?

EVIDENCE: _____

_____

EVIDENCE: _____

_____

SOURCE 2:

IN WHAT STYLE(S) IS THE MATERIAL PRESENTED?

EVIDENCE: _____

_____

EVIDENCE: _____

_____

RH.6-8.5: Describe how a text presents information (e.g., sequentially, comparatively, causally).

GRADE 8 WORKSHEETS: RH.6-8.6

NAME:

SCORE:

SOURCE 1:

POINT OF VIEW/PURPOSE:

EVIDENCE: _____

EVIDENCE: _____

SOURCE 2:

POINT OF VIEW/PURPOSE:

EVIDENCE: _____

EVIDENCE: _____

RH.6-8.6: Identify aspects of a text that reveal an author's point of view or purpose (e.g., loaded language, inclusion or avoidance of particular facts).

NAME:

SCORE:

SOURCE 1:

VISUAL ELEMENT:

HOW DOES THE VISUAL ELEMENT SUPPORT UNDERSTANDING OF THE TOPIC?

_____

_____

_____

SOURCE 2:

VISUAL ELEMENT:

HOW DOES THE VISUAL ELEMENT SUPPORT UNDERSTANDING OF THE TOPIC?

_____

_____

_____

RH.6-8.7: _Integrate visual information (e.g., in charts, graphs, photographs, videos, or maps) with other information in print and digital text_

NAME:

SCORE:

TOPIC:

VISUAL ELEMENT 1:

HOW WILL YOU USE THE ELEMENT IN YOUR REPORT?

_____

_____

VISUAL ELEMENT 2:

HOW WILL YOU USE THE ELEMENT IN YOUR REPORT?

_____

_____

VISUAL ELEMENT 3 (if needed):

HOW WILL YOU USE THE ELEMENT IN YOUR REPORT?

_____

_____

*COMPLETE YOUR REPORT/WRITING WITH THE ADDITION OF VISUAL ELEMENTS

RH.6-8.7: _SEE PAGE 1 FOR STANDARDS_

GRADE 8 WORKSHEETS: RH.6-8.8

NAME:

SCORE:

FACTUAL SOURCE:

FACT:

EVIDENCE: _____
_____

OPINION SOURCE:

OPINION:

EVIDENCE: _____
_____

REASONED JUDGEMENT SOURCE:

REASONED JUDGEMENT:

EVIDENCE: _____
_____

RH.6-8.8: Distinguish among fact, opinion, and reasoned judgment in a text.

GRADE 8 WORKSHEETS: RH.6-8.9

NAME:

SCORE:

PRIMARY SOURCE:

SECONDARY SOURCE:

SIMILARITIES:

DIFFERENCES:

WHICH SOURCE IS MORE EFFECTIVE? WHY?

RH.6-8.9: Analyze the relationship between a primary and secondary source on the same topic.

GRADE 8 WORKSHEETS: RH.6-8.10

NAME: _____   SCORE: _____

HISTORY/SOCIAL STUDIES TEXT: **TOPIC(S):**

#1 _____   _____

HISTORY/SOCIAL STUDIES TEXT: **TOPIC(S):**

#2 _____   _____

HISTORY/SOCIAL STUDIES TEXT: **TOPIC(S):**

#3 _____   _____

HISTORY/SOCIAL STUDIES TEXT: **TOPIC(S):**

#4 _____   _____

HISTORY/SOCIAL STUDIES TEXT: **TOPIC(S):**

#5 _____   _____

HISTORY/SOCIAL STUDIES TEXT: **TOPIC(S):**

#6 _____   _____

HISTORY/SOCIAL STUDIES TEXT: **TOPIC(S):**

#7 _____   _____

RH.6-8.10: *By the end of grade 8, read and comprehend history/social studies texts in the grades 6-8 text complexity band independently and proficiently.*

SCIENCE & TECHNICAL SUBJECTS

GRADE 8 STANDARDS

SCIENCE & TECHNICAL SUBJECTS

Key Ideas and Details:

CCSS.ELA-LITERACY.RST.6-8.1

Cite specific textual evidence to support analysis of science and technical texts.

CCSS.ELA-LITERACY.RST.6-8.2

Determine the central ideas or conclusions of a text; provide an accurate summary of the text distinct from prior knowledge or opinions.

CCSS.ELA-LITERACY.RST.6-8.3

Follow precisely a multistep procedure when carrying out experiments, taking measurements, or performing technical tasks.

Craft and Structure:

CCSS.ELA-LITERACY.RST.6-8.4

Determine the meaning of symbols, key terms, and other domain-specific words and phrases as they are used in a specific scientific or technical context relevant to *grades 6-8 texts and topics*.

CCSS.ELA-LITERACY.RST.6-8.5

Analyze the structure an author uses to organize a text, including how the major sections contribute to the whole and to an understanding of the topic.

CCSS.ELA-LITERACY.RST.6-8.6

Analyze the author's purpose in providing an explanation, describing a procedure, or discussing an experiment in a text.

GRADE 8 STANDARDS

SCIENCE & TECHNICAL SUBJECTS

Integration of Knowledge and Ideas:

CCSS.ELA-LITERACY.RST.6-8.7

Integrate quantitative or technical information expressed in words in a text with a version of that information expressed visually (e.g., in a flowchart, diagram, model, graph, or table).

CCSS.ELA-LITERACY.RST.6-8.8

Distinguish among facts, reasoned judgment based on research findings, and speculation in a text.

CCSS.ELA-LITERACY.RST.6-8.9

Compare and contrast the information gained from experiments, simulations, video, or multimedia sources with that gained from reading a text on the same topic.

Range of Reading and Level of Text Complexity:

CCSS.ELA-LITERACY.RST.6-8.10

By the end of grade 8, read and comprehend science/technical texts in the grades 6-8 text complexity band independently and proficiently.

GRADE 8 WORKSHEETS: RST.6-8.1

NAME:

SCORE:

SOURCE:

KEY CONCEPT(S): _____

_____

_____

TEXT EVIDENCE: _____

_____

TEXT EVIDENCE: _____

_____

TEXT EVIDENCE: _____

_____

TEXT EVIDENCE: _____

_____

RST.6-8.1: Cite specific textual evidence to support analysis of science and technical texts.

NAME:

SCORE:

SOURCE:

KEY CONCEPT(S): _____

_____

_____

SUMMARY: _____

_____

_____

_____

_____

_____

_____

_____

_____

RST.6-8.2: Determine the central ideas or conclusions of a text; provide an accurate summary of the text distinct from prior knowledge or opinions.

NAME:

SCORE:

PROCEDURE:

STEPS:

#1 _____

_____

#2 _____

_____

#3 _____

_____

#4 _____

_____

#5 _____

_____

#6 _____

MEASUREMENTS/DATA/COMMENTS: _____

_____

_____

RST.6-8.3: Follow precisely a multistep procedure when carrying out experiments, taking measurements, or performing technical tasks.

GRADE 8 WORKSHEETS: RST.6-8.4

NAME:

SCORE:

SYMBOL/KEY TERM:

SOURCE:

DEFINITION:

SYMBOL/KEY TERM:

SOURCE:

DEFINITION:

SYMBOL/KEY TERM:

SOURCE:

DEFINITION:

RST.6-8.4: Determine the meaning of symbols, key terms, and other domain-specific words and phrases as they are used in a specific scientific or technical context relevant to grades 6-8 texts and topics.

SOURCE 1:

HOW IS THE TEXT ORGANIZED? _____

_____

HOW DOES THIS HELP THE READER TO UNDERSTAND THE TOPIC? _____

_____

_____

SOURCE 2:

HOW IS THE TEXT ORGANIZED? _____

_____

HOW DOES THIS HELP THE READER TO UNDERSTAND THE TOPIC? _____

_____

_____

RST.6-8.5: *Analyze the structure an author uses to organize a text, including how the major sections contribute to the whole and to an understanding of the topic.*

PROCEDURE/EXPERIMENT:

AUTHOR'S PURPOSE:

EVIDENCE: _____

_____

EVIDENCE: _____

_____

EXPLANATION:

AUTHOR'S PURPOSE:

EVIDENCE: _____

_____

EVIDENCE: _____

_____

RST.6-8.6: *Analyze the author's purpose in providing an explanation, describing a procedure, or discussing an experiment in a text.*

NAME:

SCORE:

SOURCE 1:

VISUAL ELEMENT:

HOW DOES THE VISUAL ELEMENT SUPPORT UNDERSTANDING OF THE TOPIC?

_____

_____

_____

SOURCE 2:

VISUAL ELEMENT:

HOW DOES THE VISUAL ELEMENT SUPPORT UNDERSTANDING OF THE TOPIC?

_____

_____

_____

RST.6-8.7: *Integrate quantitative or technical information expressed in words in a text with a version of that information expressed visually (e.g., in a flowchart, diagram, model, graph, or table).*

NAME:

SCORE:

TOPIC:

VISUAL ELEMENT 1:

HOW WILL YOU USE THE ELEMENT IN YOUR REPORT?

_____

_____

VISUAL ELEMENT 2:

HOW WILL YOU USE THE ELEMENT IN YOUR REPORT?

_____

_____

VISUAL ELEMENT 3 (if needed):

HOW WILL YOU USE THE ELEMENT IN YOUR REPORT?

_____

_____

*COMPLETE YOUR REPORT/WRITING WITH THE ADDITION OF VISUAL ELEMENTS

RST.6-8.7: _SEE PAGE 1 FOR STANDARDS_

GRADE 8 WORKSHEETS: RST.6-8.8

NAME:

SCORE:

FACTUAL SOURCE:

FACT:

EVIDENCE:

SPECULATIVE SOURCE:

SPECULATION:

EVIDENCE:

REASONED JUDGEMENT SOURCE:

REASONED JUDGEMENT:

EVIDENCE:

RST.6-8.8: *Distinguish among facts, reasoned judgment based on research findings, and speculation in a text.*

NAME:

SCORE:

MULTIMEDIA SOURCE:

TEXT SOURCE:

SIMILARITIES:

DIFFERENCES:

WHICH SOURCE IS MORE EFFECTIVE? WHY?

RST.6-8.9: *Compare and contrast the information gained from experiments, simulations, video, or multimedia sources with that gained from reading a text on the same topic.*

GRADE 8 WORKSHEETS: RH.6-8.10

NAME: **SCORE:**

SCIENCE/TECHNICAL TEXT: **TOPIC(S):**

#1 _____   _____

SCIENCE/TECHNICAL TEXT: **TOPIC(S):**

#2 _____   _____

SCIENCE/TECHNICAL TEXT: **TOPIC(S):**

#3 _____   _____

SCIENCE/TECHNICAL TEXT: **TOPIC(S):**

#4 _____   _____

SCIENCE/TECHNICAL TEXT: **TOPIC(S):**

#5 _____   _____

SCIENCE/TECHNICAL TEXT: **TOPIC(S):**

#6 _____   _____

SCIENCE/TECHNICAL TEXT: **TOPIC(S):**

#7 _____   _____

RH.6-8.10: By the end of grade 8, read and comprehend science/technical texts in the grades 6-8 text complexity band independently and proficiently.

RATIOS & PROPORTIONAL RELATIONSHIPS

GRADE 8 STANDARDS

RATIOS & PROPORTIONAL RELATIONSHIPS

THERE ARE NO 8TH GRADE STANDARDS FOR THIS SECTION

THE
NUMBER
SYSTEM

THE NUMBER SYSTEM

Know that there are numbers that are not rational, and approximate them by rational numbers:

CCSS.MATH.CONTENT.8.NS.A.1

Know that numbers that are not rational are called irrational. Understand informally that every number has a decimal expansion; for rational numbers show that the decimal expansion repeats eventually, and convert a decimal expansion which repeats eventually into a rational number.

CCSS.MATH.CONTENT.8.NS.A.2

Use rational approximations of irrational numbers to compare the size of irrational numbers, locate them approximately on a number line diagram, and estimate the value of expressions (e.g., π2). *For example, by truncating the decimal expansion of √2, show that √2 is between 1 and 2, then between 1.4 and 1.5, and explain how to continue on to get better approximations.*

NAME:

SCORE:

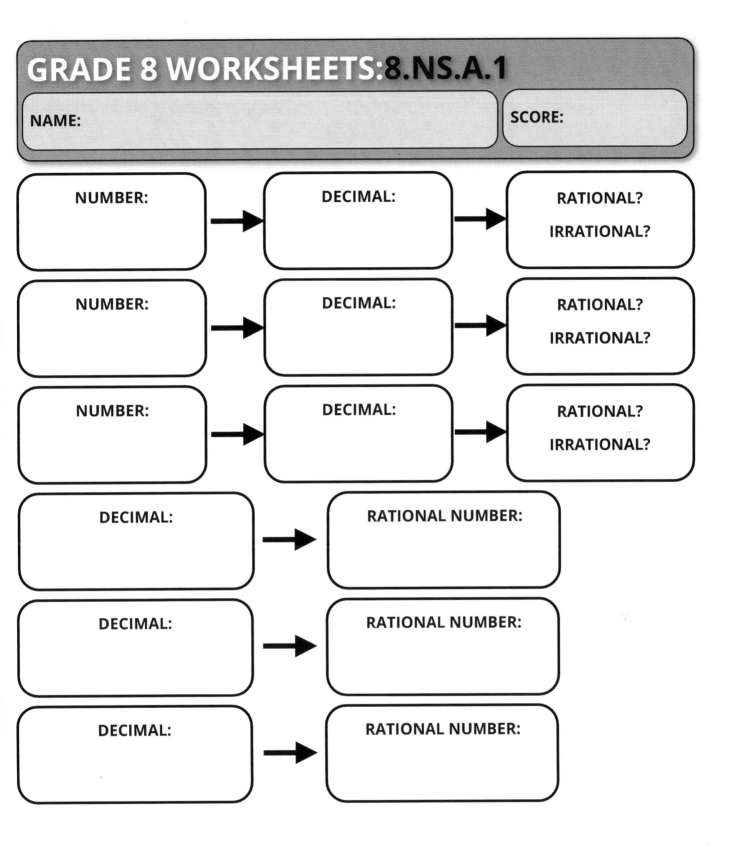

NUMBER: → DECIMAL: → RATIONAL? IRRATIONAL?

NUMBER: → DECIMAL: → RATIONAL? IRRATIONAL?

NUMBER: → DECIMAL: → RATIONAL? IRRATIONAL?

DECIMAL: → RATIONAL NUMBER:

DECIMAL: → RATIONAL NUMBER:

DECIMAL: → RATIONAL NUMBER:

8.NS.A.1: *Know that numbers that are not rational are called irrational. Understand informally that every number has a decimal expansion; for rational numbers show that the decimal expansion repeats eventually, and convert a decimal expansion which repeats eventually into a rational number.*

GRADE 8 WORKSHEETS:8.NS.A.2

NAME:

SCORE:

NUMBER LIST:

DECIMAL APPROXIMATIONS:

GRAPH THE NUMBERS ON THE NUMBER LINE:

EXPLAIN HOW TO MAKE THE GRAPH OF NUMBERS MORE ACCURATE:

_____

_____

_____

_____

8.NS.A.2: Use rational approximations of irrational numbers to compare the size of irrational numbers, locate them approximately on a number line diagram, and estimate the value of expressions (e.g., π2). For example, by truncating the decimal expansion of √2, show that √2 is between 1 and 2, then between 1.4 and 1.5, and explain how to continue on to get better approximations.

EXPRESSIONS
& EQUATIONS

EXPRESSIONS & EQUATIONS

Expressions and Equations Work with radicals and integer exponents:

CCSS.MATH.CONTENT.8.EE.A.1

Know and apply the properties of integer exponents to generate equivalent numerical expressions. For example, $3^2 × 3^{-5} = 3^{-3} = 1/3^3 = 1/27$.

CCSS.MATH.CONTENT.8.EE.A.2

Use square root and cube root symbols to represent solutions to equations of the form $x^2 = p$ and $x^3 = p$, where p is a positive rational number. Evaluate square roots of small perfect squares and cube roots of small perfect cubes. Know that $\sqrt{2}$ is irrational.

CCSS.MATH.CONTENT.8.EE.A.3

Use numbers expressed in the form of a single digit times an integer power of 10 to estimate very large or very small quantities, and to express how many times as much one is than the other. *For example, estimate the population of the United States as 3 times 10^8 and the population of the world as 7 times 10^9, and determine that the world population is more than 20 times larger.*

CCSS.MATH.CONTENT.8.EE.A.4

Perform operations with numbers expressed in scientific notation, including problems where both decimal and scientific notation are used. Use scientific notation and choose units of appropriate size for measurements of very large or very small quantities (e.g., use millimeters per year for seafloor spreading). Interpret scientific notation that has been generated by technology

EXPRESSIONS & EQUATIONS

Understand the connections between proportional relationships, lines, and linear equations:

CCSS.MATH.CONTENT.8.EE.B.5

Graph proportional relationships, interpreting the unit rate as the slope of the graph. Compare two different proportional relationships represented in different ways. For example, compare a distance-time graph to a distance-time equation to determine which of two moving objects has greater speed.

CCSS.MATH.CONTENT.8.EE.B.6

Use similar triangles to explain why the slope m is the same between any two distinct points on a non-vertical line in the coordinate plane; derive the equation $y = mx$ for a line through the origin and the equation $y = mx + b$ for a line intercepting the vertical axis at b.

EXPRESSIONS & EQUATIONS

Analyze and solve linear equations and pairs of simultaneous linear equations:

CCSS.MATH.CONTENT.8.EE.C.7

Solve linear equations in one variable.

CCSS.MATH.CONTENT.8.EE.C.7.A

Give examples of linear equations in one variable with one solution, infinitely many solutions, or no solutions. Show which of these possibilities is the case by successively transforming the given equation into simpler forms, until an equivalent equation of the form $x = a$, $a = a$, or $a = b$ results (where a and b are different numbers).

CCSS.MATH.CONTENT.8.EE.C.7.B

Solve linear equations with rational number coefficients, including equations whose solutions require expanding expressions using the distributive property and collecting like terms.

CCSS.MATH.CONTENT.8.EE.C.8

Analyze and solve pairs of simultaneous linear equations.

• CCSS.MATH.CONTENT.8.EE.C.8.A

Understand that solutions to a system of two linear equations in two variables correspond to points of intersection of their graphs, because points of intersection satisfy both equations simultaneously.

• CCSS.MATH.CONTENT.8.EE.C.8.B

Solve systems of two linear equations in two variables algebraically, and estimate solutions by graphing the equations. Solve simple cases by inspection. *For example, 3x + 2y = 5 and 3x + 2y = 6 have no solution because 3x + 2y cannot simultaneously be 5 and 6.*

• CCSS.MATH.CONTENT.8.EE.C.8.C

Solve real-world and mathematical problems leading to two linear equations in two variables. *For example, given coordinates for two pairs of points, determine whether the line through the first pair of points intersects the line through the second pair.*

GRADE 8 WORKSHEETS: 8.EE.A.1

NAME:

SCORE:

EXPONENT EXPRESSION:

SIMPLIFY:

EXPONENT EXPRESSION:

SIMPLIFY:

EXPONENT EXPRESSION:

SIMPLIFY:

8.EE.A.1: *Know and apply the properties of integer exponents to generate equivalent numerical expressions. For example, $3^2 \times 3^{-5} = 3^{-3} = 1/3^3 = 1/27$.*

GRADE 8 WORKSHEETS:8.EE.A.2

NAME:

SCORE:

SQUARE ROOT: → SOLUTION:

CUBE ROOT: → SOLUTION:

SQUARE ROOT: → SOLUTION:

CUBE ROOT: → SOLUTION:

SQUARE ROOT: → SOLUTION:

CUBE ROOT: → SOLUTION:

8.EE.A.2: *Use square root and cube root symbols to represent solutions to equations of the form $x^2 = p$ and $x^3 = p$, where p is a positive rational number. Evaluate square roots of small perfect squares and cube roots of small perfect cubes. Know that $\sqrt{2}$ is irrational.*

NAME:

SCORE:

STORY/PROBLEM:

NUMBER TO POWER OF 10:

STORY/PROBLEM:

NUMBER TO POWER OF 10:

STORY/PROBLEM:

NUMBER TO POWER OF 10:

STORY/PROBLEM:

NUMBER TO POWER OF 10:

8.EE.A.3: *Use numbers expressed in the form of a single digit times an integer power of 10 to estimate very large or very small quantities, and to express how many times as much one is than the other. For example, estimate the population of the United States as 3 times 10^8 and the population of the world as 7 times 10^9, and determine that the world population is more than 20 times larger.*

NAME:

SCORE:

STORY/PROBLEM:

ANSWER IN SCIENTIFIC NOTATION:

STORY/PROBLEM:

ANSWER IN SCIENTIFIC NOTATION:

STORY/PROBLEM:

ANSWER IN SCIENTIFIC NOTATION:

8.EE.A.4: *Perform operations with numbers expressed in scientific notation, including problems where both decimal and scientific notation are used. Use scientific notation and choose units of appropriate size for measurements of very large or very small quantities (e.g., use millimeters per year for seafloor spreading). Interpret scientific notation that has been generated by technology*

NAME:

SCORE:

DATA SET 1:

UNIT RATE 1:

EQUATION 1:

DATA SET 2:

UNIT RATE 2:

EQUATION 2:

COMPARE THE TWO EQUATIONS/DATA SETS:

_____

_____

_____

_____

_____

8.EE.B.5: *Graph proportional relationships, interpreting the unit rate as the slope of the graph. Compare two different proportional relationships represented in different ways. For example, compare a distance-time graph to a distance-time equation to determine which of two moving objects has greater speed.*

GRADE 8 WORKSHEETS: 8.EE.B.6

NAME:

SCORE:

ORDERED PAIRS:

ABC	X	Y

$y = mx + b$

PROVE MATHEMATICALLY THAT THE SLOPE IS CONSTANT:

_____

_____

_____

_____

_____

8.EE.B.6: *Use similar triangles to explain why the slope m is the same between any two distinct points on a non-vertical line in the coordinate plane; derive the equation y = mx for a line through the origin and the equation y = mx + b for a line intercepting the vertical axis at b.*

NAME:

SCORE:

LINEAR EQUATION & WORK SPACE:

SOLUTION(S):

LINEAR EQUATION & WORK SPACE:

SOLUTION(S):

LINEAR EQUATION & WORK SPACE:

SOLUTION(S):

8.EE.C.7.A: *Solve linear equations in one variable. Give examples of linear equations in one variable with one solution, infinitely many solutions, or no solutions. Show which of these possibilities is the case by successively transforming the given equation into simpler forms, until an equivalent equation of the form x = a, a = a, or a = b results (where a and b are different numbers).*

8.EE.C.7.B: *Solve linear equations with rational number coefficients, including equations whose solutions require expanding expressions using the distributive property and collecting like terms.*

NAME:

SCORE:

LINEAR EQUATION:

CONVERT & SOLVE:

LINEAR EQUATION:

CONVERT & SOLVE:

LINEAR EQUATION:

CONVERT & SOLVE:

8.EE.C.7.A-B: SEE PAGE 1 FOR STANDARDS AND EXPECTATIONS

NAME:

SCORE:

EQUATION 1 POINTS:

ABC	X	Y

EQUATION 2 POINTS:

ABC	X	Y

WORK SPACE:

EQUATION 1:

EQUATION 2:

INTERSECTION:

(,)

8.EE.C.8.A: *Analyze and solve pairs of simultaneous linear equations. Understand that solutions to a system of two linear equations in two variables correspond to points of intersection of their graphs, because points of intersection satisfy both equations simultaneously.*

NAME:

SCORE:

WORK SPACE:

ABC	X	Y

EQUATION 1:

EQUATION 2:

8.EE.C.8.B: Solve systems of two linear equations in two variables algebraically, and estimate solutions by graphing the equations. Solve simple cases by inspection. For example, 3x + 2y = 5 and 3x + 2y = 6 have no solution because 3x + 2y cannot simultaneously be 5 and 6.

GRADE 8 WORKSHEETS: 8.EE.C.8.C

NAME:

SCORE:

ABC	X	Y

EQUATION 1:

EQUATION 2:

DESCRIBE WHICH LINES PASS THROUGH WHICH POINTS:

_____

_____

_____

_____

8.EE.C.8.C: Solve real-world and mathematical problems leading to two linear equations in two variables. For example, given coordinates for two pairs of points, determine whether the line through the first pair of points intersects the line through the second pair.

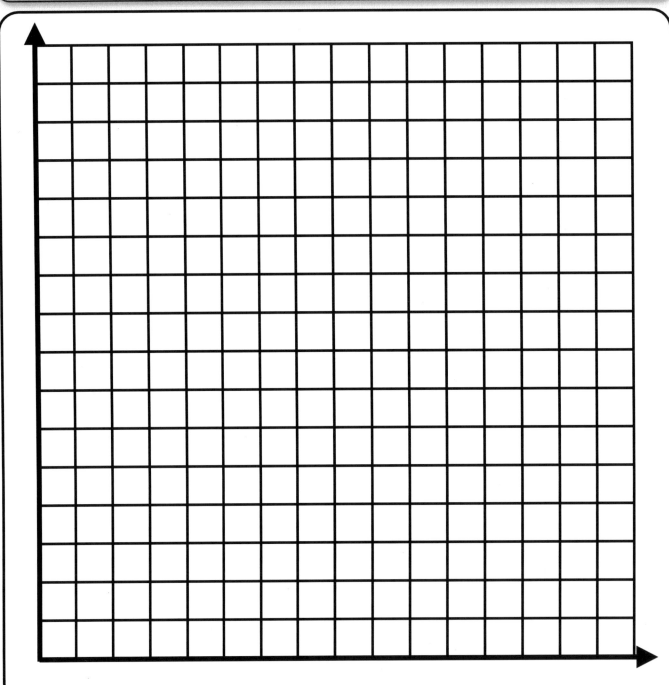

GRADE 8 WORKSHEETS: GRAPH PAPER 2

NAME:

SCORE:

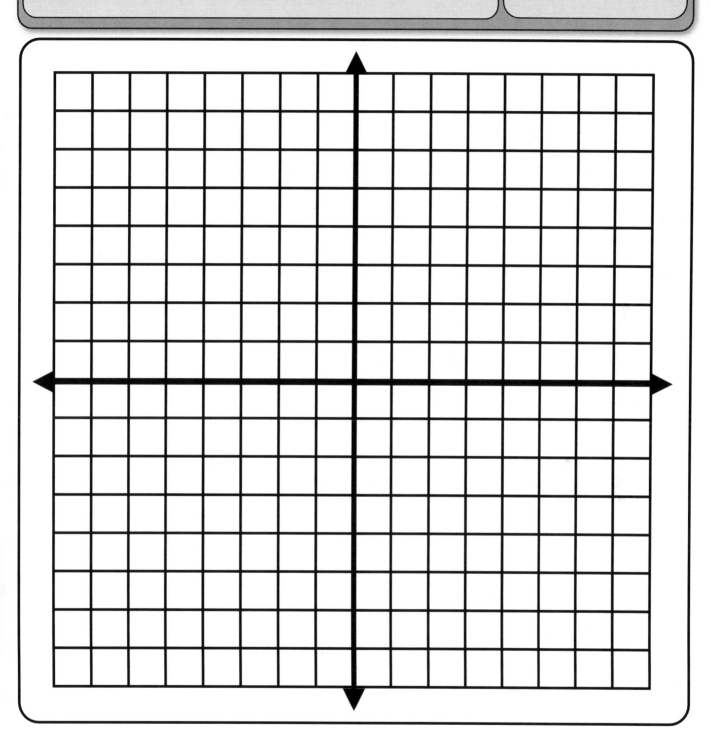

NAME:

SCORE:

ABC	X	Y

WORK SPACE:

FUNCTIONS

FUNCTIONS

Define, evaluate, and compare functions:

CCSS.MATH.CONTENT.8.F.A.1

Understand that a function is a rule that assigns to each input exactly one output. The graph of a function is the set of ordered pairs consisting of an input and the corresponding output.1

CCSS.MATH.CONTENT.8.F.A.2

Compare properties of two functions each represented in a different way (algebraically, graphically, numerically in tables, or by verbal descriptions). *For example, given a linear function represented by a table of values and a linear function represented by an algebraic expression, determine which function has the greater rate of change.*

CCSS.MATH.CONTENT.8.F.A.3

Interpret the equation $y = mx + b$ as defining a linear function, whose graph is a straight line; give examples of functions that are not linear. *For example, the function A = s2 giving the area of a square as a function of its side length is not linear because its graph contains the points (1,1), (2,4) and (3,9), which are not on a straight line.*

FUNCTIONS

Use functions to model relationships between quantities:

CCSS.MATH.CONTENT.8.F.B.4

Construct a function to model a linear relationship between two quantities. Determine the rate of change and initial value of the function from a description of a relationship or from two (*x*, *y*) values, including reading these from a table or from a graph. Interpret the rate of change and initial value of a linear function in terms of the situation it models, and in terms of its graph or a table of values.

CCSS.MATH.CONTENT.8.F.B.5

Describe qualitatively the functional relationship between two quantities by analyzing a graph (e.g., where the function is increasing or decreasing, linear or nonlinear). Sketch a graph that exhibits the qualitative features of a function that has been described verbally.

NAME:

SCORE:

FUNCTION FORMULA:

INPUT	FUNCTION	OUTPUT

WORK SPACE:

8.F.A.1: *Understand that a function is a rule that assigns to each input exactly one output. The graph of a function is the set of ordered pairs consisting of an input and the corresponding output.*

NAME:

SCORE:

FUNCTION 1:

FUNCTION 2:

FUNCTION 1 DATA:

INPUT	FUNCTION	OUTPUT

FUNCTION 2 DATA:

INPUT	FUNCTION	OUTPUT

DESCRIBE THE DIFFERENCES IN THE SHAPES OR GRAPHS OF THE FUNCTIONS:

_____

_____

_____

_____

8.F.A.2: *Compare properties of two functions each represented in a different way (algebraically, graphically, numerically in tables, or by verbal descriptions). For example, given a linear function represented by a table of values and a linear function represented by an algebraic expression, determine which function has the greater rate of change.*

NAME:

SCORE:

LINEAR FUNCTION:

NON-LINEAR FUNCTION:

FUNCTION 1 DATA:

INPUT	FUNCTION	OUTPUT

FUNCTION 2 DATA:

INPUT	FUNCTION	OUTPUT

DESCRIBE THE DIFFERENCES IN THE SHAPES OR GRAPHS OF THE FUNCTIONS:

_____

_____

_____

_____

8.F.A.3: *Interpret the equation $y = mx + b$ as defining a linear function, whose graph is a straight line; give examples of functions that are not linear. For example, the function $A = s2$ giving the area of a square as a function of its side length is not linear because its graph contains the points (1,1), (2,4) and (3,9), which are not on a straight line.*

NAME:

SCORE:

GRAPH YOUR LINEAR & NON-LINEAR FUNCTIONS:

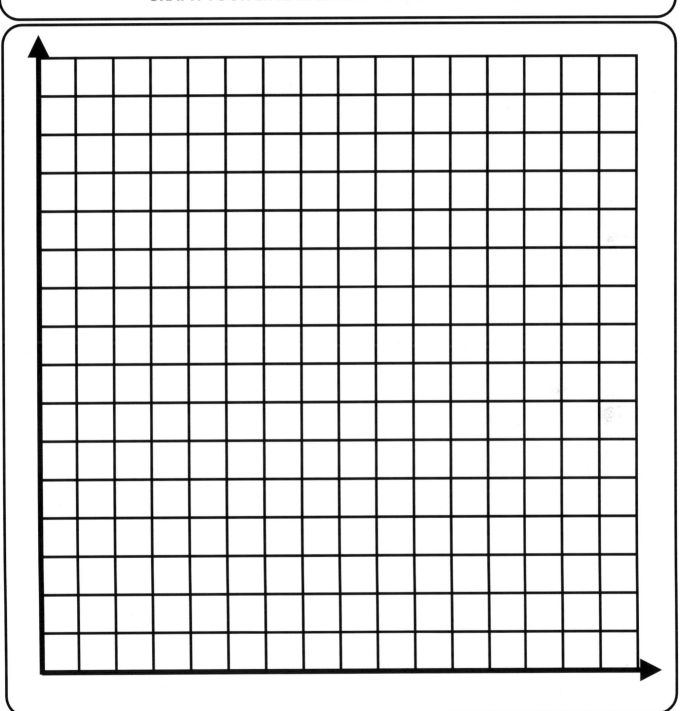

8.F.A.3: *SEE PAGE 1 FOR STANDARDS AND EXPECTATIONS*

GRADE 8 WORKSHEETS:8.F.B.4

NAME:

SCORE:

STORY/PROBLEM:

FUNCTION FORMULA:

DATA TABLE:

INPUT	FUNCTION	OUTPUT

8.F.B.4: *Construct a function to model a linear relationship between two quantities. Determine the rate of change and initial value of the function from a description of a relationship or from two (x, y) values, including reading these from a table or from a graph. Interpret the rate of change and initial value of a linear function in terms of the situation it models, and in terms of its graph or a table of values.*

GRADE 8 WORKSHEETS:8.F.B.5

NAME:

SCORE:

DESCRIPTION OF FUNCTION:

FORMULA:

8.F.B.5: *Describe qualitatively the functional relationship between two quantities by analyzing a graph (e.g., where the function is increasing or decreasing, linear or nonlinear). Sketch a graph that exhibits the qualitative features of a function that has been described verbally.*

GEOMETRY

GEOMETRY

Understand congruence and similarity using physical models, transparencies, or geometry software:

CCSS.MATH.CONTENT.8.G.A.1

Verify experimentally the properties of rotations, reflections, and translations:

- CCSS.MATH.CONTENT.8.G.A.1.A

Lines are taken to lines, and line segments to line segments of the same length.

- CCSS.MATH.CONTENT.8.G.A.1.B

Angles are taken to angles of the same measure.

- CCSS.MATH.CONTENT.8.G.A.1.C

Parallel lines are taken to parallel lines.

CCSS.MATH.CONTENT.8.G.A.2

Understand that a two-dimensional figure is congruent to another if the second can be obtained from the first by a sequence of rotations, reflections, and translations; given two congruent figures, describe a sequence that exhibits the congruence between them.

CCSS.MATH.CONTENT.8.G.A.3

Describe the effect of dilations, translations, rotations, and reflections on two-dimensional figures using coordinates.

CCSS.MATH.CONTENT.8.G.A.4

Understand that a two-dimensional figure is similar to another if the second can be obtained from the first by a sequence of rotations, reflections, translations, and dilations; given two similar two-dimensional figures, describe a sequence that exhibits the similarity between them.

CCSS.MATH.CONTENT.8.G.A.5

Use informal arguments to establish facts about the angle sum and exterior angle of triangles, about the angles created when parallel lines are cut by a transversal, and the angle-angle criterion for similarity of triangles. *For example, arrange three copies of the same triangle so that the sum of the three angles appears to form a line, and give an argument in terms of transversals why this is so.*

GRADE 8 STANDARDS

GEOMETRY

Understand and apply the Pythagorean Theorem:

CCSS.MATH.CONTENT.8.G.B.6

Explain a proof of the Pythagorean Theorem and its converse.

CCSS.MATH.CONTENT.8.G.B.7

Apply the Pythagorean Theorem to determine unknown side lengths in right triangles in real-world and mathematical problems in two and three dimensions.

CCSS.MATH.CONTENT.8.G.B.8

Apply the Pythagorean Theorem to find the distance between two points in a coordinate system.

Solve real-world and mathematical problems involving volume of cylinders, cones, and spheres:

CCSS.MATH.CONTENT.8.G.C.9

Know the formulas for the volumes of cones, cylinders, and spheres and use them to solve real-world and mathematical problems.

GRADE 8 WORKSHEETS: 8.G.A.1.A-C

NAME:

SCORE:

CONFIRM THAT THE SHAPE(S) ARE STILL CONGRUENT WITH MEASURES:

ORIGINAL SHAPE:

SHAPE AFTER

ROTATION/REFLECTION/TRANSLATION:

ORIGINAL SHAPE MEASURES:

NEW SHAPE MEASURES:

8.G.A.1.A: *Verify experimentally the properties of rotations, reflections, and translations: Lines are taken to lines, and line segments to line segments of the same length.*

8.G.A.1.B: *Angles are taken to angles of the same measure.*

8.G.A.1.C: *Parallel lines are taken to parallel lines.*

NAME:

SCORE:

CONFIRM THAT THE SHAPE(S) ARE STILL CONGRUENT:

ORIGINAL SHAPE:

SHAPE AFTER

ROTATION/REFLECTION/TRANSLATION:

EXPLAIN/PROVE WHY THE SHAPES ARE STILL CONGRUENT:

_____

_____

_____

_____

8.G.A.2: *Understand that a two-dimensional figure is congruent to another if the second can be obtained from the first by a sequence of rotations, reflections, and translations; given two congruent figures, describe a sequence that exhibits the congruence between them.*

NAME:

SCORE:

ORIGINAL SHAPE:

MODIFIED SHAPE:

EXPLAIN/PROVE WHY THE SHAPES ARE STILL CONGRUENT:

_____

_____

_____

_____

_____

8.G.A.3: *Describe the effect of dilations, translations, rotations, and reflections on two-dimensional figures using coordinates.*

GRADE 8 WORKSHEETS:8.G.A.4

NAME:

SCORE:

FIND THE SIMILARITIES BETWEEN THE FIGURES:

FIGURE 1:

FIGURE 2:

EXPLAIN/PROVE WHY THE SHAPES ARE SIMILAR:

____

____

____

____

8.G.A.4: *Understand that a two-dimensional figure is similar to another if the second can be obtained from the first by a sequence of rotations, reflections, translations, and dilations; given two similar two-dimensional figures, describe a sequence that exhibits the similarity between them.*

NAME:

SCORE:

ILLUSTRATION OF PYTHAGOREAN THEOREM:

ARGUMENT/PROOF:

_____

_____

_____

_____

_____

_____

_____

8.G.B.6: _Explain a proof of the Pythagorean Theorem and its converse._

ILLUSTRATION OF CONVERSE OF PYTHAGOREAN THEOREM:

ARGUMENT/PROOF:

_____

_____

_____

_____

_____

_____

8.G.B.6: *SEE PAGE 1 FOR STANDARDS AND EXPECTATIONS*

NAME:

SCORE:

PROBLEM:

ILLUSTRATION:

SOLUTION/WORK SPACE:

8.G.B.7: Apply the Pythagorean Theorem to determine unknown side lengths in right triangles in real-world and mathematical problems in two and three dimensions.

GRADE 8 WORKSHEETS: 8.G.B.8

NAME:

SCORE:

PROBLEM:

DATA TABLE:

ABC	X	Y

SOLUTION/WORK SPACE:

8.G.B.8: *Apply the Pythagorean Theorem to find the distance between two points in a coordinate system.*

NAME:

SCORE:

PROBLEM:

FORMULA(S):

ILLUSTRATION:

SOLUTION/WORK SPACE:

8.G.C.9: *Know the formulas for the volumes of cones, cylinders, and spheres and use them to solve real-world and mathematical problems.*

STATISTICS & PROBABILITY

STATISTICS & PROBABILITY

Investigate patterns of association in bivariate data:

CCSS.MATH.CONTENT.8.SP.A.1

Construct and interpret scatter plots for bivariate measurement data to investigate patterns of association between two quantities. Describe patterns such as clustering, outliers, positive or negative association, linear association, and nonlinear association.

CCSS.MATH.CONTENT.8.SP.A.2

Know that straight lines are widely used to model relationships between two quantitative variables. For scatter plots that suggest a linear association, informally fit a straight line, and informally assess the model fit by judging the closeness of the data points to the line.

CCSS.MATH.CONTENT.8.SP.A.3

Use the equation of a linear model to solve problems in the context of bivariate measurement data, interpreting the slope and intercept. *For example, in a linear model for a biology experiment, interpret a slope of 1.5 cm/hr as meaning that an additional hour of sunlight each day is associated with an additional 1.5 cm in mature plant height.*

CCSS.MATH.CONTENT.8.SP.A.4

Understand that patterns of association can also be seen in bivariate categorical data by displaying frequencies and relative frequencies in a two-way table. Construct and interpret a two-way table summarizing data on two categorical variables collected from the same subjects. Use relative frequencies calculated for rows or columns to describe possible association between the two variables. *For example, collect data from students in your class on whether or not they have a curfew on school nights and whether or not they have assigned chores at home. Is there evidence that those who have a curfew also tend to have chores?*

NAME:

SCORE:

QUESTION/PROBLEM:

DATA SET 1:

	VALUE

DATA SET 2:

	VALUE

GRAPH THE DATA:

WHAT CONCLUSIONS/INFERENCES CAN YOU MAKE ABOUT THE DATA?

_____

_____

8.SP.A.1: *Construct and interpret scatter plots for bivariate measurement data to investigate patterns of association between two quantities. Describe patterns such as clustering, outliers, positive or negative association, linear association, and nonlinear association.*

NAME:

SCORE:

QUESTION:

	VALUE

GRAPH THE DATA & DRAW A BEST-FIT LINE FOR DATA:

EXPLAIN THE ACCURACY OF YOUR LINE AND HOW IT FITS THE DATA:

_____

_____

_____

8.SP.A.2: *Know that straight lines are widely used to model relationships between two quantitative variables. For scatter plots that suggest a linear association, informally fit a straight line, and informally assess the model fit by judging the closeness of the data points to the line.*

NAME:

SCORE:

PROBLEM:

DATA TABLE:

ABC	X	Y

LINEAR EQUATION:

EXPLAIN WHAT THE SLOPE AND INTERCEPT MEAN IN THIS SITUATION:

8.SP.A.3: Use the equation of a linear model to solve problems in the context of bivariate measurement data, interpreting the slope and intercept. For example, in a linear model for a biology experiment, interpret a slope of 1.5 cm/hr as meaning that an additional hour of sunlight each day is associated with an additional 1.5 cm in mature plant height.

NAME:

SCORE:

DATA BEING GRAPHED:

CONSTRUCT A TWO-WAY TABLE:

			TOTALS
TOTALS			

DESCRIBE THE ASSOCIATIONS BETWEEN THE VARIABLES:

_____

_____

_____

8.SP.A.4: *Understand that patterns of association can also be seen in bivariate categorical data by displaying frequencies and relative frequencies in a two-way table. Construct and interpret a two-way table summarizing data on two categorical variables collected from the same subjects. Use relative frequencies calculated for rows or columns to describe possible association between the two variables. For example, collect data from students in your class on whether or not they have a curfew on school nights and whether or not they have assigned chores at home. Is there evidence that those who have a curfew also tend to have chores?*

ABOUT THE AUTHOR

Andrew Frinkle is an award-nominated teacher and writer with experience in America and overseas. He has taught PreK all the way up to adult classes, and has focused on ESOL and EFL techniques. With a young child at home now, he's been developing more and more teaching strategies and books aimed at helping young learners.

His many educational works include:

• 50 STEM Labs & 50 More STEM Labs

• Common Core Assessment Templates

• Common Core Vocabulary Cards

• Graph Paper Math

• How to Draw with Basic Shapes

• Science Now!

• Sentence Builders & Word Builders

• Weekly Sentence Strips

• Story Starters

• Movers and Shakers & the Expansion Sets

• Basic Skills Workbooks: Alphabet Skills, Number Sense, and Shapes

• Monster Zoo Math

• Dealing With Archetypical Children - A Classroom Management Resource

• How to Draw Comic Books

• ***Get this and other books on Amazon, Lulu, and other online booksellers!***

Read more about Andrew Frinkle at www.underspace.org. He also maintains the educational websites www.littlelearninglabs.com and www.common-core-assessments.com. He also works full time for www.havefunteaching.com and its affiliated sites, as well as writing fantasy and science fiction novels under the pen name Velerion Damarke.

23651325R10091

Made in the USA
Columbia, SC
10 August 2018